Why Are You So Beautiful, Our Precious Angel?

Poems honouring our son, Aiden
by
Susan Milne

Why Are You So Beautiful, Our Precious Angel?

All Rights Reserved

Copyright © 2020 Susan Milne

Reproduction in any manner, in whole or in part,
in English or any other language, or otherwise,
without the written permission of the copyright holder is
prohibited

For information address mickiedaltonbooks@lycos.com

First Printing 2020

ISBN: 978-0-6485470-9-9

Published by The Mickie Dalton Foundation
NSW
Australia

About the Author

Susan Milne, was a proud mother of three, with a typical, joyful family life until tragedy struck. This, her first book is an uncensored journey through a mother's darker moments. She is currently residing in Melbourne's outer Eastern Suburbs with her husband and two daughters.

Acknowledgements

I would like to thank my husband and daughters, for patiently and lovingly encouraging me while I wrote this book. My parents showed their love and support for Aiden, by coming over one day a week or more to spend time with him. They visited Aiden every single time he was in hospital, for his wide variety of different illnesses, or at times to adjust his anti-seizure medications. Our son was loved and comforted by both grandparents whenever possible and we greatly acknowledge that. Aiden's Grandmother called him often on the phone and was very loving and supportive. Aiden's grandparents did visit him but they found it hard to watch him physically deteriorate. I will be forever grateful to them for their unconditional love for their grandchild.

I give thanks to Lisa and her children. Lisa would scratch his head and lie down with him, on his bed while I was making lunch. She also visited him in hospital on a number of occasions. Her loving children would willingly go into our room and spend time with him, before socialising with our daughters. That was a very considerate thing that they did.

My deep gratitude is extended to Stan, Wendy and Shirley for their moral support, both during the journey with us and after his passing. I would like to express my deep appreciation to Phillip for his consistent encouragement and reliability, as well as regular visits to our house, with or without his wife who also had cancer at the time.

It was a blessing that Alison came from Queensland to be there for the funeral, which took her more than seventeen hours to arrive at our place. She did not stay with us as we were still too fragile for much company, but she came over the next day to support us and ended up staying for lunch before the long drive home.

Last but not least, I would like to express my gratitude to our friends from the church who took care of the needs of our other two children and willingly looked after them, whenever we asked them to. We really appreciated the prayers, cards and moral support from our church that supported Aiden as much as they could. Thousands of people were praying for his recovery.

There are gorgeous people that I have not mentioned who have supported us, through phone conversations and flowers, among other things. My sincere gratitude goes out to those I have and have not mentioned.

Why are You so Beautiful, Our Precious Angel?

Introduction:

I had never heard my father swear or seen him cry, until our whole world as we knew it was turned upside down, by the catastrophic diagnosis of an innocent little boy, who had done nothing to deserve this life sentence. All dad could manage to say was "OH SHIT" as I was holding him while he openly cried, not caring who was watching and witnessing his grief.

Our daughters had been staying with their Grandparents for a few days, so that we could focus all of our attention on our son. They both had totally different reactions but their faces were red from exhaustion and tears that we should have been able to wipe away. There were no words that could be said to comfort them at this heartbreaking time.

I'll never forget what one daughter asked us without even thinking about what she said. "Is my brother going to die?" I wanted to shelter her and protect her from hearing the worst possible outcome. I wanted to tell her all the things that I wanted and needed to believe. A very big part of me would not and could not accept what was being said. This was extremely hard to process.

I saw past her tears and studied her body language for a moment, not sure of what to say. Her posture and defiant look in her eyes, told me that she was demanding and expecting the truth. I wanted to tell her that the doctors would both give him chemotherapy and then operate or within the month, surgery would be performed on her brother, taking the tumour out of his brain.

Why are You so Beautiful, Our Precious Angel?

At that moment I became aware that she had the strength and maturity about her, in certain areas that was way beyond her years. We thought that this was hard, but it was only the beginning of our heartbreaking journey.

Aiden was diagnosed on the fifteenth of January, 2009 with a brain tumour, otherwise known as a hypothalamic ependymoma. Later on we were informed that it was much to our astonishment and shock, cancerous. Brain tumours are a very rare form of cancer. A neurologist at the hospital said that he was probably born with it, or it developed when he was only a few months old.

It started off as a slow growing tumour but by the time it was discovered, not only was it growing rapidly, but it was the size of a golf ball. The tumour was located really deep in his brain, between the hypothalamus gland and the pituitary gland. Aiden was only nine years old when he died.

Words cannot express how frustrating and difficult it was, not only for Aiden to go through this for two and a half years, but as parents who had to watch helplessly as our child deteriorated over time and had frequent stays in hospital.

Let's not trivialise how hard it was for our two remaining daughters, who not only lovingly, passionately supported their brother through this, but did not always get the attention and time spent with us that they needed and deserved. They bear no resentment or grudge towards us because of circumstances beyond anyone's control.

It was a long drawn out process and something I would have willingly traded my own good health for if that opportunity had been given to me. I hope that while reading this book you'll get a bit of an insight as to what our gorgeous son's personality was like. Our lives and those who knew and loved our boy were richly blessed by his presence.

There is no greater loss then having to bury your own child.

There can be no stronger feeling of survivors' guilt, than that of a loving grandparent.

I would like to dedicate this book to a number of people, however there are too many to mention individually. This book is dedicated to anybody who has lost a child, not just through cancer, but tragic circumstances. Parents are not meant to bury their own children, irrespective of if it was somebody who was raising their own family or a fifty year old. It's something that is devastating, but through time, you can recover from it and enjoy life again.

On a more personal note, I would like to include both sets of grandparents who suffered alongside of us, as they deeply loved and adored our little boy. Last but not least, I would like to dedicate this book to our son Aiden, who was the best son any parent would be proud to have had the opportunity to raise.

Chapter One
Through Innocent Eyes

Shock Diagnosis

My son's left arm made me scared as it trembled a lot. Try as I might I couldn't will it to stop. For the second time in one month, Aiden had a severe case of gastritis. Unfortunately that was the least of everyone's problems.

When he had an MRI and a Cat Scan the results were not what we would have planned. My boy who last month scaled six foot high fences and such, was diagnosed with a brain tumour. The reality of the situation hurt way too much.

Into the Intensive Care Unit we went.

When I saw Aiden with all these tubes coming out of his head, I wished he had the flu, so we could take him home and put him to bed.

My son was to stay in an induced coma for one week. This made me so stressed I was unable to get enough sleep. My daughters and parents were crying so much. Even the ministers from our church found it tough.

Before his three weeks at hospital were up, he had a shunt in the back of his head and a port on the side of his body, in line with his armpit. We were unaware at the time that the port would be accessed quite a bit. From that day forth I'm not going to pretend. My son's climbing days had come to an abrupt end.

To rest in the love and peace of Jesus is to have the endurance to face the trials, knowing that he always keeps his promises, and that nothing can separate us from the love of God. Jesus I pray for strength for today as I rest in you.

Matthew 11 verses 29-30 (NIV)

29: "Take my yoke upon you and learn of me; for I am meek and lowly in heart: and you will find rest for your souls. For my yoke is easy and my burden is light"

I Don't Want to Go

I didn't want to go home while our son lay in an induced coma. I thought my husband and daughters would be alright on their own. I could ring them on the phone sometimes, to touch base with how our boy was.

I was told you can't sleep here all week because you have such a long battle ahead of you. Listen to us as experts in our field in what we are telling you, you have to do. Your husband and children need you home at night right now. You'll have to trust us that we know what we're talking about, somehow.

But I was unaware of the long process that lay ahead of me. As far as I was concerned, my child was sick and he needed me there in case he woke up. That was the only reality I was able to see.

My son has been sick for a long time, I sadly thought. It took every ounce of energy that I had to leave the hospital at night. I felt so frustrated and sad. I felt really bad, as leaving him there did not seem fair. It was like neglecting my child and leaving him alone. There was nothing more I could do but leave because he couldn't communicate with me. Aiden wasn't well enough to come home.

I could not stay home.
I did not want him to feel alone.
Back to the hospital I went to stay for a while.
I was told there was a long road ahead of me.
I was told I should be with my family.
They were right because our girls loved their brother
But they really needed their mother.

Jesus I thank you for the comfort you give as we turn to you and hand over the control of every difficult situation. I thank you for the doctors and nurses who looked after our child, but he was your child first, because you created him. I thank you also for the loving support of my family through his illness.

Isiah 41v10 (NIV)

"So do not fear, for I am with you; do not be dismayed, for I am your God. I will strengthen you and help you; I will uphold you with my righteous right hand."

Prayers and Support

I had called some friends from the church, to organise group prayers. Two people came over after we arrived home from hospital to show how much they cared. It was late at night, and we were still in shock as we had only just found out about his brain tumour that day, which made me feel incredibly fatigued, and for a few minutes, I entertained the thought of telling them politely to just go away.

This lovely lady that I rang must have contacted other people, because she felt it was urgent that they knew what they needed to do. Talk to God and Jesus on our behalf and gain some loving support from the Holy Spirit too.

Four people at least had been praying together, as from my understanding, they were going to continue doing that with their families as well. I believe they would have come over even if it was hailing or stormy weather. They both have children at home of their own. They had left them with their husbands, so as to support George and me. I was grateful that someone outside of the family would be willing to see what the best ways were to support our family.

They came to bring peace. They came to offer love. They chose to come over to our house that day, the purpose of which was to sit with God and pray. Throughout his whole illness, they supported and cared, they comforted, shared, opened their homes to our beautiful girls, offered hospitality, loved our family and were there whenever we needed them.

Throughout our whole journey these people were always looking after our children when needed, and praying for us and supporting us as our spiritual sisters in Christ. They gave true meaning to the words part of the church body.

Jesus, I thank you for placing it on their hearts to come over and pray for us. I thank you for beautiful friends, and for the love that you show us through the love that your children give, who are part of the body of Christ.

1 Corinthians 12v27-28 (NIV)

"Now you are the body of Christ, and each one of you is a part of it. And in the church God has appointed first of all the apostles, second prophets, third teachers, then workers of miracles, also those having gifts of healing, those able to help others, those with gifts of administration, and those speaking in different kinds of tongues.

John 14 verse 27 (NIV)

"Peace I leave with you; my peace give you. I do not give you as the world gives. Do not let your hearts be troubled and do not be afraid."

Independent Spirit

It was time for him to be brought out of his induced coma so he could go to another hospital room. I contacted my husband and asked him if he could buy some pull-ups for him to use. He informed me that he would meet me at the hospital soon.

When our boy came out of his induced coma, it was such a relief to us. There had been such a huge build up of stress. We had to remain strong, but emotionally I was in a complete mess.

"Daddy brought you some special undies that you can wee in," I said.

He looked at me as if to say, "You can put those nappies in the bin today." Our independent boy just quietly said, "Aiden's a big boy. Nappies are for babies."

He wanted the bottle to wee in instead.

Why Are You So Beautiful, Our Precious Angel?

For the rest of the stay, until it was time to go home, irrespective of whether it was the social worker there or if he was alone with his mum or dad, he used a bottle or got on the toilet if it was what he chose to do.

I sat there sadly thinking, *I wish that mummy could go through this instead of you.*

My son was showing me something he knew I needed to see.
He was independent, innocent, young and carefree.
He was not worried.
So why should we be?
Our souls needed peace to feel free.

Jesus I thank you that he was so independent. I am grateful that he was focused on maintaining his independence and that you gave him peace. I put my trust in you Lord.

Proverbs 3 verse 5-7 (NIV)
"Trust in the Lord with all your heart and lean not on your own understanding; in all your ways acknowledge Him and He will make your paths straight."

Bad News

Keep his body at a certain angle his surgeons daily said. I wished he would cooperate and do as he was told, so that we could go home earlier instead. For roughly two weeks Aiden had these revolting lifesaving tubes, dangling from his head. It didn't matter to him who visited, or if he was being fed. My son was determined not to sit still for very long. To see my active boy confined to the hospital

Why Are You So Beautiful, Our Precious Angel?

bed, so frustrated and bored, felt so wrong.

Once I placed his very full wee bottle outside his room, something I soon learnt I couldn't do and I very soon regretted it. My son seized his golden opportunity and jumped out of bed. I was gone for less than a minute. I was amazed that he didn't yank the tubes out of his head. That's what he was like in the hospital room. My independent boy's face would soon swell up like a balloon. This was caused by the large amounts of steroids I got him to swallow. He innocently did just as he was told to do. I wish I could take them for him, so that the side effects were not something he had to go through. We knew that it was the brain tumour, but that was all we were told. We had our first group meeting with his specialists and may I be so bold as to say, I had trouble processing all that was said.

They told us that it was cancerous, this horrible tumour in my son's head. George supportively held my hand as I cried. He was shocked and upset but he remained strong, as he kept a lot of his emotions inside. I felt angry, confused, traumatised and really sad. This was the start of many more group meetings to come. I'd look at them sometimes and wish they would all go away. I didn't want to hear any more bad news on that day.

The social worker was there to offer moral and financial support. I am grateful and thankful that there were lots of times when we were given petrol vouchers to ease the financial burden of the constant trips back and forth from the hospital. I am also grateful that they always made us feel welcome there. There was always someone there to advocate in our behalf if there was ever a problem. They involved us in his care, and taught us how to look after him as much as possible, so that we did not have to rely on the nurses as much. One of the nurses there had photos in her room of herself with the children of the cancer unit. She smiled at Aiden and was always nice to him. On the odd occasion that he swore, she would laugh or smile. There were always positive things happening amongst all the trauma we went through.

I thank you Jesus for all the support that was available for us, which included financial support and camps for our other daughters to attend and loving supportive nurses and doctors. I thank you for loving us through an incredible difficult trial, not just personally but also the way that other people were used by you to show us your heart and your love.

Isiah 57v15 (NIV)

"For this is what the most high and lofty one says he who lives lives forever, whose name is holy: "I live in a high and holy place, but also with him who is contrite and low in spirit, to revive the spirit of the lowly and to revive the heart of the contrite."

Why Are You So Beautiful, Our Precious Angel?

Seizures

I looked at our child, so sick in our bed.
I wished I could take it away from him and take on his suffering instead.
Our boy struggled and fought, as he was seizing and seizing.
His body was burning, and he had a lot of trouble breathing.
Our daughters were in and out of our room.
I had called the ambulance, so hopefully they would be here very soon.
My husband and I supported Aiden through his discomfort and pain.
It was late at night and I was so tired that I could cry
I looked at him sadly not understanding why
our whole family had to watch him go through this
This was the first seizures that he had
To not be able to stop them made me feel shocked and sad.

I thank you Jesus for the ambulance drivers that provided such beautiful care for Aiden. I thank you for medication to treat seizures. I thank you for the health care card which took away the financial burden of having to find the money to pay for the many ambulance trips to the hospital, throughout our journey. I thank you that our Medicare system is so good.

Philipians4v6-7 (NIV)

"Do not be anxious about anything, but in everything by prayer and supplication with thanksgiving let your requests be made known to God. And the peace of God, which surpasses all understanding, will guard your hearts and your minds in Christ Jesus."

Why Are You So Beautiful, Our Precious Angel?

Calmness Placid Behaviour

I love how gentle soft and caring you are
I love how you don't worry about tomorrow
You're not sad about the shattered dreams you can't follow
I love how you don't complain
still laugh and appreciate each day
You are grateful whenever people visit
or go out of their way to do something nice for you
Since you got sick your personality has changed
I love you so much
But today I'm grieving and missing the way you were
It's not that I would say which side of your personality I prefer.
It's just that I really miss you the way you were.
I can honestly say that your illness is out of my power and beyond my control.
I'm missing the way you ran into my arms for cuddles.
I'm missing the way you smiled and snuggled.
I'm missing the way you used to help your dad collect logs for the fire.
I'm missing your independence.
You were so happy and active before we knew you were so sick
I'm missing you squirting Windex on the windows
And the way you used to vacuum the floorboards.
I'm missing you, being able to daily show me
The creative things that you do.
I've never known a child to be so glad, to be
Going outside to do gardening with his dad.
I'm missing believing that I had a healthy boy to raise.

Why Are You So Beautiful, Our Precious Angel?

Sometimes life gets so hard I feel like I'm walking around in a daze.

I'm missing you being well enough to sleep in your bed.
I love our night-time cuddles and feeling our gorgeous boy beside me.
But I wish things could go back to normal, so that your dad
Could cuddle me in bed instead.

Jesus I am grieving because I am missing the way that Aiden was. I am sad because he is so sick. Jesus I know that you are a merciful God and that you love Aiden more than I do. I ask you to give me the strength to get through today. I need to feel your peace.

Psalm 116 verse 1-2 (NIV)

"I love the Lord, for he heard my voice;
he heard my cry for mercy. Because he turned his ear to me, I will call on him as long as I live."

Innocent Support and Love

I watched with great sadness, my daughter lying down.
Aiden was with her, showing how much he loved and cared for her.
Her pretty forehead was creased up in a frown.

That sums up the beautiful, thoughtful,
respectful, caring child that he was.

The pain in her head was so bad.
He was supporting her, as he did
with the family, and those that he loved.
Our son was much sicker,
yet he showed her how much empathy he had.

Our children comforted each other a lot. The pain was as bad for them as it was for him, because they were powerless to be able to protect him from it. The love that they had for him, increased his quality of life, and gave him a reason to smile, and a feeling of being loved.

Jesus I thank you that he had the empathy to be able to lie down with his sister when she was sick and put her needs of his own. That is a gift that he had, which you gave to him, to carry her burden, when she was sick. I thank you also for my other two children who are a gift from you. I pray that they draw close to you as you love them more than I ever could.

Galatians 6v2 (NIV)

"Carry each other's burdens, and in this way you will fulfil the law of Christ."

Why Are You So Beautiful, Our Precious Angel?

Innocent Questions

Aiden never complained about the tumour in his head.
He never cried and threw tantrums
because he was so sick
He never once said: It's not fair that I have to spend so
much time in bed.

He rarely got angry as the tumour started to grow.
When he did it did not last long as he was able to quickly
let it go.
His innocence and trust really began to show
and it made me so sad I wanted to cry
when he asked me
"Why do I have a tumour in my head?
Do you want it?"

"Yes," I said, "so that you can no longer have it."
George said, "No, but I'd like to feed it to the worms
instead."
I want to take this away from you,
so that your sickness can come to a complete end.
How do you answer a question like that
From a child who was developmentally two or three?
I don't understand and I can't comprehend
But I knew Jesus loved Aiden,
My family and me.

There was the presence
of Jesus in his eyes
It's only human to cry

But his strength made me never
question if God and Jesus
was and is alive
I saw Jesus the Holy Spirit too
in a lot of things he would say behave and do

There is a lot he taught me about
Gentle words respect kindness love
An innocent faith. An innocent child

Jesus I ask you to protect us as a family, physically, emotionally, spiritually, mentally and in every way. Jesus I ask you to be with other people who are supporting and caring for their child who has a terminal illness, and that they and their families can be protected physically, emotionally, spiritually, mentally and in every way also.

I remember lying down in bed with Aiden that day and we heard a frog croaking outside. George went out and brought it in, so he could look at it. The frog jumped on his pillow and Aiden laughed. It felt good to hear him laugh and see him smile.

1 Peter 5:7 (NIV)

"Cast all your anxiety on him because he cares for you."

Why Are You So Beautiful, Our Precious Angel?

My Son's Loving Touch

I took my child to Mainly Music because he loved it so much
Yet despite all the side effects from the treatment to his cancer
I could still feel the gentleness of his loving touch
"I'm going to kiss you and make you better," he said as he watched the tears run down my face He had a bald head from the chemotherapy and a cushionoid face from the steroids

Aiden was comforting me
and he was meant to be enjoying this place
Mainly music was the only place
I could go with him because of his age
He was too sick to go to school
What did it matter if he was
older than the other children at this stage?
In between hospital visits
we still had good times
We still went to church
had cuddles and he laughed and had fun
Family and friends were welcomed
warmly by our special one

There is no more beautiful gift from God that you can receive then the love and affection from an innocent child. It was as though Jesus had entered into his heart and comforted me through his soul.

Why Are You So Beautiful, Our Precious Angel?

Psalm 127 verse 3 (NIV)

"Sons are a heritage from the Lord, children a reward from him."

Why Don't They Recognise Me?

On one of Aiden's better days,
when he had the strength to go out for a few hours
we went to the indoor playground together.
I just wished he could have better days
and I would know he would get better forever.
I celebrated with him, on his special day.
Before we played in the indoor playground,
there was something he wanted to do.
I was concerned it might make him sad,
so it was something I wanted to protect him from going through.

Back to his old school for half an hour we went.
His old best friend was heaven sent.
I don't know exactly where to begin to try and explain,
how devastated I felt, when none of his close friends recognised him.

The last time he was at the special development school,
he had blond hair and blue eyes.
Aiden might have just as easily gone as someone else in disguise.
He was twenty two kilograms heavier, and didn't look like,
the child and best friend that they'd met earlier.
His hair was short, brown, curly too.
There was nothing I could physically do

Why Are You So Beautiful, Our Precious Angel?

to shelter or protect him,
as he had completely changed in personality as well.
I was physically unable to make them understand
that this was the same child.
His old best friend didn't mind.
Out of everybody she was the most kind.

These were her friends as well.
They all played and talked, but she instinctively knew,
and had the empathy, maturity and understanding
that was well beyond her years Without her actions, it
would have brought me to tears
In her heart she knew what she wanted to do
She decided not to play with her friends
but to step aside and spend time with Aiden
I saw the love of Jesus
through her gentleness,
kindness and respect to our son
and it's something I will never ever forget
Aiden really tried to let her know that this was the same
boy inside.
They played alongside each other.
They no longer had the closeness of a sister and a brother
they no longer interacted as best friends but more like
cousins who rarely saw each other.

It gave Aiden a little comfort on that day.
When his old best friend and he had a little play.
His old best friend did not care
if he had blonde or brown curly hair
She was happy to play with him

Why Are You So Beautiful, Our Precious Angel?

She showed me a little of who
The Father Son and Holy Spirit is
by accepting him loving him
for who he was

Looking back now I don't know if you were born with a brain tumour or if it developed early on in life The point is I made the
most of the time spent with you
There were lots of things I could do
to improve your quality of life
God made you beautiful
just the way you are
I greatly appreciate the gift
he gave us which was you
Your faith has kept you strong
You are right where you belong.

Jesus I thank you that the young girl treated Aiden the way that she would like to be treated, with respect, compassion, kindness and empathy.

Matthew 7v12 (NIV)

"So in everything, do to others what you would have them do to you, for this sums up the Law and the Prophets."

Psalm 46 verse 1 (NIV)

"God is our refuge and strength, an ever- present help in trouble"

Why Are You So Beautiful, Our Precious Angel?

Look Into His Eyes

Aiden went with his dad to visit his Neurologist that day.
I decided to stay home and pray.
She said, "His reflexes are gone,
and he will need to have an emergency MRI tonight."
After careful consideration, and a lot of different opinions,
we decided that it would be alright.

When we spoke to the people at
the hospital they said,
"Don't worry, the Emergency Department are aware of the situation."
I wondered why she could look at him and not let us through
Telling us to go to the MRI department is what would have been better for her to do
We arrived at the Emergency Department, expecting to just go through.
I went to the front and was told, "There's nothing more we can do.
You'll just have to take your place in the queue."
I stood there and watched, parents with able bodied children.
I watched the people behind the desk talking to them
While our son was overtired and could not keep his head straight
I did not understand why we were told to wait

I was also told: "If you want what is best for your son
Just wait as your turn will come"

Why Are You So Beautiful, Our Precious Angel?

Inside I was crying, as my heart was breaking
My husband said words that I dare not repeat.
Security was called, because I was so distressed
and the person behind the desk was grounded in her seat
She was so cold as she disregarded our need
The pain was so bad it felt like an eternal bleed

I met a security guard outside and when I told him what we were going through
I needed somebody calmer then myself to tell me what to do
I didn't need to be here there was another section that I needed to get to. I thanked him with relief as my son would soon rest.

There were two reasons that we were so upset. The first reason was because we were told that the emergency department would be aware of the urgency of the MRI.

The second reason was that Aiden was so overtired, so there was an increased risk of him having a seizure. I wanted to protect him from having one.

Jesus I repent for holding onto anger about the whole situation in emergency

I thank you Jesus that he never had a seizure despite having to stay at the hospital for so long and that we were able to take him home that night, so that he could sleep with us. I am grateful that the security guard recognised that there was nothing personal behind our reactions, and that he understood that we were only trying to advocate for our son, advocate for his needs, and get him the medical help that he needed. I am also grateful that he showed empathy and compassion for us, and made allowances for us, and showed us direction in the help we needed. I thank you Jesus for your unconditional love as the Holy Spirit was working for us.

Colossians 3 v13-14 (NIV)

"Bear with each other and forgive whatever grievances you may have against one another. Forgive as the Lord forgave you. And of all these virtues put on love which binds them all together in perfect unity."

That Treasured Kiss

Not long before we knew how sick Aiden was
he had had an intellectual disability test
The reason for this was because
he had improved so much. The results meant that he was able to go to a special school.

I took him there in a wheelchair
feeling like it was unfair
that our boy was terminally ill
I wanted to do something to make him feel good
Take his mind of his pain
I wanted him to feel happy again
Aiden would have liked to go back to the physical health he once had
Aiden did not understand why he could not spend time with the friends that he had had
It was something that made both of us feel sad

Why Are You So Beautiful, Our Precious Angel?

This was the last time he was at the special school
and a beautiful boy gave him a kiss
If I were to ever see that boy again I would say
something to him like this:

"That kiss on the cheek made Aiden feel like he had a
friend in the room."
Unbeknown to us he was going to die very soon
It was a pleasant memory that he had.

I could count the amount of times he went to that school on
one hand.
That's okay, because that young child would not have had
the ability to understand
what a significant thing he did on that day.

Aiden did not understand why he could not remain,
in the school where he first made lots of friends.
It's strange how children do beautiful things without
knowing.
Before experiences take away their innocence, as they
are still growing.
That one small kiss gave my son something to treasure,
and for a short time,
gave Aiden a feeling of acceptance and pleasure.

What a blessing, that children do things out of innocence, support and love. This boy knew not what he did. I am grateful and thankful for the love he felt from an innocent child. It reinforces to me of God's unconditional love as Aiden smiled and focused on what was positive. His gratitude reinforced to me that he loved Jesus who was right by his side. Knowing how strong his faith was, comforted me through his illness and gave me strength to move forward after he died.

Matthew 18v3-4 (NIV)

"And he said: I tell you the truth, unless you change and become like little children, you will never enter the kingdom of heaven. Therefore whoever humbles himself like this child is the greatest in the kingdom of heaven."

Why Are You So Beautiful, Our Precious Angel?

The Difficult Goodbyes

I drove down to Ballarat, which took a few hours.
When I arrived I admired my aunt's beautiful flowers.
The purpose of my visit was to see my uncle
for the last time, while he was alive.
My aunt would be one day alone,
with no children or grandchildren.
How would she deal with this, and later on thrive
with her husband no longer alive?

Several times that day, the mobile phone started ringing.
I wished it was because my son
wanted to show off with his singing.
"I've had a lot of spit," my son continually said.
This meant that he was having a lot of seizures in bed.
It affected my visit in quite a profound way.
In spite of my favourite uncles terminal illness,
I had to make this a really short stay.
I was torn between saying goodbye to my uncle,
and spending time with my sick son.
To be torn apart like this, was not
the way things should have been done.

My parents, who had travelled up with me
on that day, accepted my decision
They knew I had to get home soon,
so we just made this a short stay.
What a blessing to be able a get a lift to my aunt and
uncle's house

to say goodbye for the last time
While we there my Uncle said things
which made me laugh.
Made me smile
Through all the sad times
To see the funny side of things with him
made me smile for a little while
It was sad I could not be both with him
and this child of mine
But seasons come and seasons go
I believe I will see my Uncle in
heaven you know

It was sad that I had to choose between spending time with Aiden and seeing my Uncle for the last time. I believe I will see my Uncle again in heaven.

Jesus I lift my Aunt up to you and I ask you to give her peace, and that she can develop an even closer relationship with you, then she already has.

I pray also for my Uncle, that he will know that he is never alone, because you are carrying his burdens.

Psalm 62 verse 5 (NIV)

"Find rest, O my soul, in God alone; my hope comes from him."

Why Are You So Beautiful, Our Precious Angel?

There and Back Again

As a family, we never knew when you would end up
staying for a week
in hospital, or be in your own comfortable home.
The strain of going back and forth made us very defensive
and sensitive.

At least when Aiden wasn't in the house, our girls
got the one on one attention they deserved.
But having our boy home was something, we much rather
preferred.
In the beginning our daughters spent a lot of time in the
Starlight Room
As they grew up, the novelty of that wore out pretty soon
It took our daughters a long time to get accustomed to
having a sick brother
So when he did go to hospital they really missed each other

He got shingles, pneumonia twice and seizures, which we
could not control.
When he kept asking me to take him home, it
left me with a gaping hole.
I often brought food from home, so he could have a break
from the hospital food.
The doctors and specialists did their best, but there were
times there was nothing
they could do, to ease the suffering which he had to go
through.

Through chemotherapy, our son got wounds on his bum.
That was the main reason he had to stop the chemotherapy,
before he had completed his treatment.

Why Are You So Beautiful, Our Precious Angel?

It wasn't fair that he had to go through this
As a parent, you're supposed to protect your children and make everything all right.
To watch helplessly, as at his young and tender age, Aiden get sick way too much,
was tough and it felt at times like it was way too much to bear.
It took a lot of energy not to cry a lot in front of him.
I was so upset because of how devoted to him I was, and because of how much I cared.

I couldn't make it better, take his physical ailments away, or spare him, not even for an hour.
He became so frail, that our boy was too sick to have a shower.
I washed him every morning instead.
The illness that originally started off in his head, had metastasised to his spine
and it caused so many complications that were beyond our control.
And it meant he had to spend a lot of time in bed
At times he reacted to certain anti-seizure medications, which could make his seizures worse.
Out of desperation one day I asked his Oncologist if it was possible
to put Aiden and me to sleep.
I was tired of his illness making me weep.
My mind would be eased and I would have had a lot more sleep,
if Aiden could have had the healthy parts of my brain.

I desperately wanted him to regain his health and
independence back again
But through it all
what was made clear
Our family unit remained strong
We valued everyone that was near

Jesus I thank you that Aiden felt a peace that surpassed all human understanding. I ask you to give us the strength and endurance to always look to you for understanding because your ways are not our ways.

Psalm 34v18 (NIV)
"The Lord is close to the brokenhearted and saves those who are crushed in spirit."

Why Are You So Beautiful, Our Precious Angel?

Coping With Another Loved One's Death

I'm off to Ballarat, as my uncle has just died.
At least he lived quite a bit while he was still alive.
It was hard to deal with this long day out.
I cried because my uncle had just died.
I also cried because my son was not mobile,
and in a lot of ways not happy, while he was still alive.
He will not have the loving support of a beautiful wife,
or children who love him, and stick by his side.

After I had talked about my uncle that day, I was told by
one aunt:
"You really loved him and will miss him, in a very special
way."
If she could read my mind, she would be made aware
of the complexities of emotions, that the funeral brought up
for me on that day.
My heart was torn in two being at my Uncle's funeral and
remembering his life at that moment was the best thing to
do.
My uncle's motto his beliefs
his approach to life his feelings attitudes
dealing with the illnesses and stresses of everyday living
can partly be summed up in his favourite song

*"One day at a time sweet Jesus that's all I'm asking of you
Help me today Show me the way One day at a time."*[1]

---

[1] One day at a time was written by Kris Kristofferson and Marijohn Wilkin

Jesus I thank you that Ken had such a strong relationship with you that he understood and applied the words to this song with such dedication in his life. I pray that we can all learn the value and necessity of trusting in you only for the cares of today.

Matthew 6v33-34 (NIV)
But seek first his kingdom and his righteousness, and all these things will be given to you as well. Therefore do not worry about tomorrow, for tomorrow will worry about itself. Each day has enough trouble of its own.

Loss of Independence
"One day I'm going to piss in the shower," my son very sadly said.
He wanted to shower on his own, but I told him,
to look after him, I'd stay with him instead.
I wished God and Jesus would give him the power,
to get up and walk to the bathroom, and grant
him that one small thing he requested.

"Can I wee in the shower with you?"
"Yes," he said, cheering up a bit.
"I know," I told him. "Maybe dad can wee with us too."

This made him laugh, and have a little smile.
But when reality kicked in, he was sad for a little while.
He was missing simple pleasures, which were out of his

Why Are You So Beautiful, Our Precious Angel?

reach.
The tumour was the size of a grapefruit
and it extended to his temporal nodes, which affected his balance.
It had metastasised to his spine, which was why he was unable to walk, or stand up in the shower.
A polite way of suppressing my intense desire to swear, is saying,
"Oh shoot, I wish he could poo this tumour out, like a piece of rotten fruit."

He struggled, but was unable to sit still.
The heaters went on in the bathroom,
to try and prevent him from catching a chill.
His body leant over to the left if not properly supported,
when Aiden was sitting on the toilet.

His immune system was badly compromised,
so a cold could cause him to die.
I wish that happened to me, not him I thought,
as I reluctantly started to cry.

I lay down with him, in what had become our bed,
and my son very determinedly said: "Give me back my legs."
I snuggled closer, his legs over my legs.
We couldn't wee in the shower together,
so I read books with him, which he loved instead.

Aiden still had a sense of humour. The fact that he could be so sick, yet he could still laugh and smile sometimes, and be grateful and appreciative of visitors and relatives over, meant to me that he was not alone and he knew it. It made me smile and laugh whenever he was smiling and laughing.

There was a peace that he had which surpassed all human understanding, so I knew that Jesus was carrying Aiden through his illness. Jesus I thank you that Aiden was always grateful and thankful and he always had a sense of humour.

Psalm 147v3 (NIV)
"He heals the brokenhearted and binds up their wounds."

John 11v35
"Jesus wept."

I Feel Rejected

When my mum takes me out in the wheelchair for a walk
I would really appreciate it if you would talk to me for a while
It would cheer me up if I could see you smile
I don't know if my face brings up memories of you,
painful memories that you have gone through
Maybe you're thinking of what you have to do today
Maybe you are feeling sad
Or your mind is far away
I can't talk much: Just ask you your name
and the name of your dog as well
When I'm well, I would appreciate
being blessed by having a few minutes of your time
In return, I will bless you by giving you mine.

Jesus, I thank you for loving people on the other end of the phone. I thank you for Christians that care. I thank you for supportive family, for the body of Christ behind us and most of all I thank you for your unconditional love and the sacrifices you have made so that we can have eternity with you.

Psalm 139V1-4

"Oh Lord, you have searched me and you know me. You know when I sit and when I rise; you perceive my thoughts from afar. You discern my going out and my lying down; you are familiar with my all my ways. Before a word is on my tongue you know it completely, O Lord."

Why Are You So Beautiful, Our Precious Angel?

Time Apart

My son is in Intensive Care and my husband did
a beautiful thing to show how much he cares.
I drove home after spending the night with our son
I was pleasantly surprised by what he had done
It was for Mother's Day and through the grief he was able
to see
something beautiful he could do for me

There on the bed were some bags of new clothes
I love you so much
I need you as a husband and friend
I wish Aiden was back home and well again
I want both of you home
It would be nice if we could all have a cuddle, and sleep in
our bed
I'm tired and I don't want to spend the night alone
Tonight it's your turn to spend the night in the Emergency
Department instead.

Jesus I thank you that George provided for me even though he was grieving to, I felt loved and appreciated by what he did. I thank you also for providing for all of my needs.

1 Chronicles 16v34 (NIV)

"Give thanks to the Lord for he is good; his love endures forever."

Phillipians 4v19 (NIV)

"And my God will meet all my needs according to his glorious riches in Christ Jesus."

Why Are You So Beautiful, Our Precious Angel?

Strong Bonds

I love the way you care and I value our prayers
My devotion to you is because of your loving
respectful nature that shines through
On one of your visits to us one day
my husband and I were arguing
and you still decided to stay
I don't have too many friends
who would think in a similar way.

We have been friends now for about eight years
Sometimes time goes so fast I find it hard to believe
In amongst that time my son got so sick
I was unable to do what I needed to achieve
I'll keep going because my faith
and your prayers keep me sane
As for our son he may not
live in this life for much longer
Our strong friendship will always remain

The prayer time from my friend
really kept me going
I did not feel lonely in my grief
She loved me enough to show
she cared enough to share
and to spend time in prayer

I am grateful to have Christian friends to be able to talk to, and pray with. Jesus thank you for always being there and loving me through other people to show me your love.

Why Are You So Beautiful, Our Precious Angel?

Numbers 6v24-26 (NIV)
"The lord bless you and keep you; the Lord make his face shine upon you and give you peace."

My Special Friend

I love you, my friend
You'll see this through till the end
The support that is driven
by the beautiful person that you are
makes me quite aware that you are such a star

I love you, my friend
your there for the family and especially my son
whose heart you have easily won
I love you my friend
In tough times you're there on the double
and you don't run when there's trouble
You are my strong light
that helps strengthen me with this fight

I love you, my friend
Your compassion and your love shine through
Without it sometimes I don't know what I'd do
It's an honour and a privilege
to have gotten to know you.
Especially in these hard times of strife,
when situations make me feel
like I'm being torn apart by a knife.

Why Are You So Beautiful, Our Precious Angel?

I love you my friend.
When his suffering is over
You won't run for cover.
I know you too will be grieving,
as we watch our son leaving.
There will be one less on the bed,
and one less at the table.
When push comes to shove,
with your help I am able
to keep going, because I know you are my friend.

1 John 4 verse 19 (NIV)
"We love because he first loved us"

This was written about my friend but it could just as easily been written about my family. I wanted them all to see how much they really meant to me. This was a single mum that I loved deeply. Despite the fact that she had her own troubles she was always there for us. She came and ate meals with us, visited us in hospital, came to his funeral talked with me on the phone, hugged George when she left and sang Aiden to sleep. She also loved and supported our girls. That is what real love is all about.

Chapter Two

Goodbye is not forever
I wish I knew

If I'd known this was going to be the last meal that you
would eat
I would not have given you pea and ham soup
You would have had your favourite treats
chocolate ice-cream and a freddo frog

If I'd known that in less than one month
you would be buried five feet underground
I would not have swept the floors or cleaned dirty
marks off the walls
I would have spent the whole day
with you in bed

If I'd known this would be the last day that you talked
on the phone
I'd have lain down next to you all day
I would have helped you dial the numbers you needed
to ring
You could have talked all you wanted
You wouldn't have been left alone

I wish I knew just how sick you were
I know what I would have preferred to do
I would have spent more time loving and nurturing you

Why Are You So Beautiful, Our Precious Angel?

<pre>
       Aiden was still massaged everyday
      We still had book time and cuddle times
         We still watched movies together
           I just could not and would not
                 accept he was dying
</pre>

Jesus I am struggling today with all the regrets of the things that I should have done with Aiden, because of circumstances that were beyond my control. I thank you for always being by his side, especially when I was not able to. I thank you that when I was doing household chores, and he needed me next to him, you were always there. I thank you that you were his best friend, support person and psychologist. I thank you that you are equally God and equally human. I thank you for knowing what was in his heart. I thank you for blessing us with our beautiful children.

Psalm 29V11 (NIV)

"The Lord gives strength to his people; the Lord blesses his people with peace."

Psalm 139v13-14

"For you created my inmost being; you knit me together in my mother's womb. I praise you because I am fearfully and wonderfully made; your works are wonderful, I know that full well."

Why Are You So Beautiful, Our Precious Angel?

The Close Bond

When our boy was roughly aged five
The year before he was diagnosed with a cancerous brain tumour
My daughter had time with him which improved his quality of life
The love that she was able to give helped him to really live
Something I will always appreciate
She had fun with him and it greatly increased his vocabulary
She would go into the bedroom with him and close the door
He would have laid down on the floor next to her
if that's what she asked him to do
She made up silly songs and related language
in her special way from television and shows to benefit him, such as
"What's in the box? Elmo Knows"
I know that this was fantastic for his ability to grow
The many photos and videos she took of him
did not come to a halt because he got sick
It was still important for her to keep going even when his steroids caused tremendous weight gain
It made his face change quite a bit
She filmed him with silly glasses on and captured his mischievous grin
This was her brother and she fully accepted him
Without these photos she'd taken all the way through I don't quite know what she'd do

Why Are You So Beautiful, Our Precious Angel?

She still listens to his voice at times and enjoys looking
at pictures of him
They really did love each other
My daughter and her beautiful brother
I wish that I had the hindsight to know how wise she
was for her young years
My mind was stuck with Aiden, what I wanted him to
be
I wanted him one day to be fully restored physically
and really healthy
I was so caught up in my emotions sadness and fear
That stopped me taking photos of him for nearly two
and a half years.

I appreciated the unique way she helped him with
language
laughed with him cuddled and cared
It was always such a strong
bond that they shared

The positive memories of how supportive our girls were to him kept me going. It comforted me. It reinforced to me how precious they are. He had always needed a lot of attention and even though they understood why it was not easy for them watching him deteriorate. They loved him to. They are Gods precious gift to us, and I appreciate and love them.

God I thank you for giving Sharna the gift of being able to work with young children and teaching children language.

Why Are You So Beautiful, Our Precious Angel?

Proverbs 17v6 (NIV)
"Children's children are a crown to the aged, and parents are the pride of their children."

To the Hospital Again

I stood there and watched the tears stream down my daughters face
I was wondering why circumstances meant that the ambulance had to come to our place
I picked up our daughter and carried her in to the ambulance for a minute or two
I wanted her to feel reassured and loved and know that they were doing everything they could possibly do to ease the suffering that her brother was going through
with his temperature soaring I kept him company in the ambulance that night
I was hoping he would not give up but hang around and fight
His breathing was rapid and there was a mask put on his face
My heart felt like it was breaking because I knew after the seizures his
body would be stiff again I knew that he would wake up and he would be in pain
With no ability to eat drink talk or poo he had no choice but to spend at least
one week in the Intensive Care Unit

Why Are You So Beautiful, Our Precious Angel?

His doctors Neurologists and specialists were trying to say
be prepared let go, accept he is dying. The temperatures are
caused by the tumour in his head.
We said that's not it it's because of the pneumonia instead.
All week long their words were piercing holes in my heart
but his temperatures returned to normal at least that's a
good start
Leaving hospital later on we thought we might win
Little did we know that this was just the beginning.
Even though he had trust, that's not what
you would say about the two of us. He had the right to trust
God, with his heart, mind and soul. We needed to accept
that while there was peace there was pain. Things were not
the same. There is a lot innocence teaches you about how
your heart should remain Sometimes silence says more than
a thousand words[2]
He did what we expected him to do
Keep trying keep fighting to pull through
We really wanted him to live

He could not comprehend what it meant not to forgive. The medical team often said: "If he dies we will not resuscitate him." They kept saying, "You need to accept that he's dying." "He's tired now." "He doesn't want to fight any-more."

Or something along those lines.

---

[2] "Sometimes silence says more than a thousand words" is a quote by Cristiane Serruya

I kept saying something along the lines of, "If he dies, I want him to be resuscitated."

It was not until an Asian doctor looked at me, full of compassion, empathy and love and said, "If we were to resuscitate him, all of his ribs would be broken, and he would never be able to recover from it."

Once he said that, it was a reassuring feeling that I was able to let go. I understood why they were telling us to stop expecting him to live. It was never our decision. I never stopped praying for him to recover, but I knew that I had to accept that he could not be resuscitated. Words are so important. I wish that somebody had explained that to me earlier, in a way that I could hear it.

For the first time I realised that somebody had talked to us about his dying in a way that expressed such love and empathy. I saw it in his eyes and body language. He demonstrated it by his calm voice and his patient reassurance. I could accept how wrong it would be for them to resuscitate a child who was suffering and dying.

John 3v16 (NIV)
"For God so loved the world that he gave his one and only Son, that whoever believes in him shall not perish but have eternal life."

It is a comfort to me that we have a loving God that understood how we felt, because Jesus died on the cross so that we might have a relationship with him, and that our sins would be forgiven. God understood our pain and I knew that he loved Aiden, more than we did.

Why Are You So Beautiful, Our Precious Angel?

I feel reassured that I will never be alone through my struggles, because of the unconditional love that God has for us. I have done nothing to deserve the love of Jesus, who was without sin, standing there with outstretched arms, having being mocked and beaten, with a crown of thorns on his head, as he took on the sins of the world. That is unconditional love and real grace. God understood our pain because he loved us so much that he sent his son Jesus to die for us. I can't comprehend how much God loves Aiden and I can't comprehend how much he loves my other children. I am just grateful that he does.

Why Are You So Beautiful, Our Precious Angel?

Sharna asleep at home. This was before her brother and sister were born.

George and Sharna bonding together, while we were out having dinner with friends.

Why Are You So Beautiful, Our Precious Angel?

Sharna and Jacinta playing at their Nanna and Grandpa's house.
They used to love going over there to visit.

Why Are You So Beautiful, Our Precious Angel?

Sharna, Jacinta and PC, having a group cuddle. Our cat was as friendly and loving as a dog. This was not long before Aiden was born.

Jacinta and I cuddling. This was her first day at kinder. It's beautiful to watch how quickly she is growing up.

Why Are You So Beautiful, Our Precious Angel?

Our friend Aunt Alison with Aiden. He used to love being held by her. We thought he was a perfectly healthy, normal baby.

Our friend Phil, with Sharna, Jacinta and Aiden. Aiden used to bang his head. I took him to a paediatrician, and he was diagnosed with autism. We still had no idea that he had a brain tumour.

Why Are You So Beautiful, Our Precious Angel?

George, Sharna, Jacinta and Aiden, with Nanna, Grandma and Grandad. This was for Sharna's kinder concert.

Aiden, Jacinta and me at an indoor playground near us. We had so much fun that day.

Why Are You So Beautiful, Our Precious Angel?

Aiden with his Grandpa, at the Aquarium in Queensland. Aiden loved the Aquarium and he loved his Grandparents.

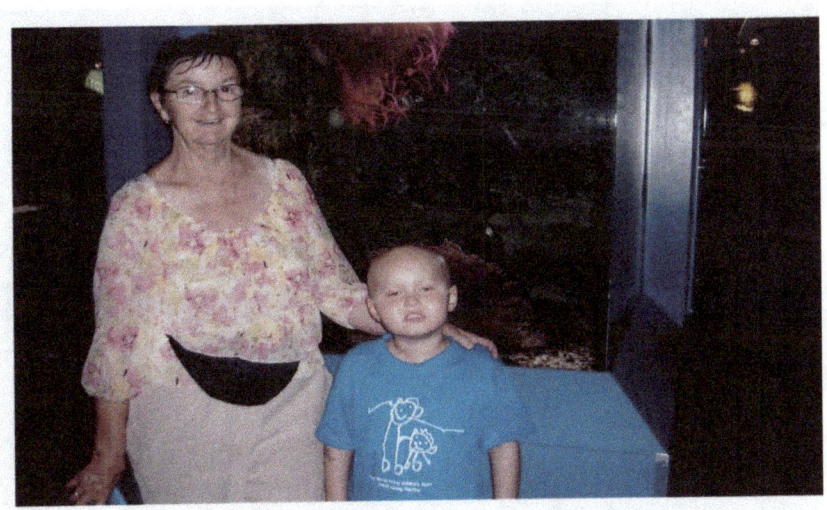

Aiden with his Nanna at the Aquarium in Queensland. They stayed with us over there, and Aiden loved that holiday. He used to jump into bed with his grandparents every morning.

Why Are You So Beautiful, Our Precious Angel?

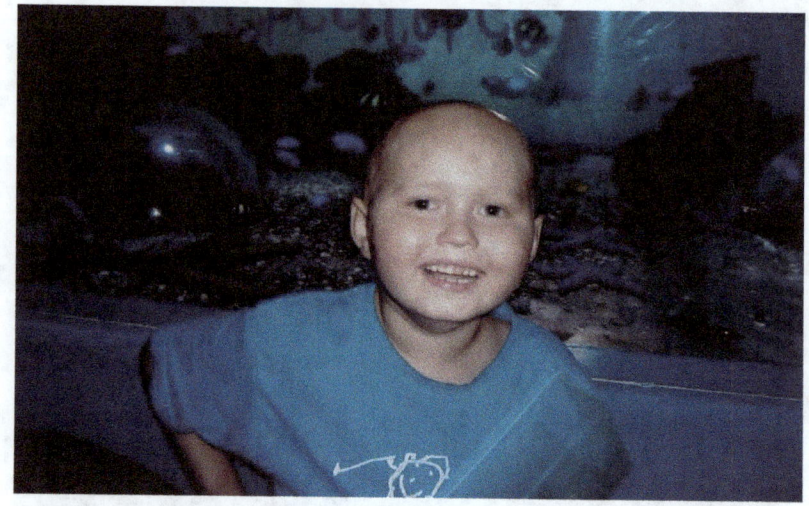

Aiden standing on his own. He used to love having his photo taken.

Why Are You So Beautiful, Our Precious Angel?

For The Last Time

For the last time you spoke to both your grandparents
on the phone
I would imagine that would make them all cry
especially when they were all alone
For the last time you enjoyed your last meal
As we kissed you again we were unaware that this was
your deal
For the last time you chose which book to read first
and let us know of your hunger and thirst
For the last time you spoke to your mum and your dad
To not hear you talk just made us feel bad
For the last time your mum and dad sat up all morning with
you in our bed
We were comforting you as you were slipping away
because of the tumour in your back and in your head
For the last time your mum dad and sisters
spent all afternoon and part of the evening in the
hospital room
Your sisters kissed cuddled and massaged you
Mum and dad had a feeling you would die very soon
For the last time your mum and dad massaged you
intermittently through the day and all through the night.
We desperately wanted you to get well and win this
fight
For the last time you opened your eyes just a bit.
It would be a gross understatement to say that it hurt
quite a bit.
Somehow we bonded more as a family in that hospital

Why Are You So Beautiful, Our Precious Angel?

room
You never know with death if it will be a long drawn
out process or the loved
ones suffering will end very soon. The trauma they
went through with their sisters'
brother reinforced to us how much we really loved
each other.

Our girls were so beautiful to him on his last night, so loving so devoted. I will always appreciate the kindness and the empathy they showed to him, because they loved him. One of our daughters played him his favourite song, which was,

"God will never stop loving me"[3]

---

[3] Karryn Henley wrote the song, "God will never stop loving me"

Why Are You So Beautiful, Our Precious Angel?

Compassion and kindness

The nurse that looked after our son
the last night he was alive was humble loving and kind
When her shift was over
She thought that we needed time at home
so that we could process our grief alone
to cope with the excruciating agony
of nurturing and supporting Aiden as he died

All night long she lovingly helped look after our son
She compassionately but firmly
encouraged us to look after each other together as one
She knew when to suction back off and jump in
She supported us individually and as a couple
The nurse was in and out all night
If we buzzed she would be there on the double

This kind lady knew he was dying
and yet she was really, really trying
to ease his suffering as much as she could
Her dark skin did not give away what nationality she was
It doesn't matter because I'm glad she was working that night
when our son finally gave up the fight
from the pneumonia kidney failure dehydration and more
Part of me died when we walked out that door
as an incomplete family unlike the night before

Why Are You So Beautiful, Our Precious Angel?

If you love someone tell them because hearts are often broken by words left unspoken

I don't know if the nurse was/is a Christian but you could see the fruits of her spirit.
She demonstrated love compassion kindness respect empathy and care
I was so grateful that she was there Her actions spoke louder than words
A more sensitive nurse we could not have seen or heard
I know that God and Jesus had their hands on our son and was with us all
the night that she died. It comforted me later on when I cried. To know how
lovingly we were all cared for when he died. The nurse showed us and him unconditional love.

Why Are You So Beautiful, Our Precious Angel?

If They Could Turn Back Time

My brothers were not able to visit Aiden
in hospital the week he died
I've got no doubt it upset them
and they and their families had their own quiet cry.

Aiden was deteriorating rapidly right before our eyes
But we loved him so much that denial hit hard
It still came as a huge unpleasant surprise when
the week was through there was nothing we could do
but cry and support each other as he died

He was so close to God There was so much peace when he died
It is our sorrow that we cried, You don't stay permanently dead
He had problems in his head I believe that he will be happy in heaven instead
I had comfort from remembering his closeness with
God, Jesus and the Holy Spirit to.
His actions and words
displayed this, throughout his whole illness, right up until he died. There was a peace, an acceptance, a sense of humour, humbleness gratitude that only came from deep faith and a love of God.

Jesus, I ask you to be with all the members of my family that loved Aiden and are grieving to. I thank you that you have always been there to support us Aiden died. Jesus I am grateful that you understand how we felt, because you to died an excruciating death, because of your love for us. Jesus, I lift up to you all those people who have lovingly nurtured their baby, child or teenager, through the sad journey of death.

Romans 8v28

"And we know that in all things God works for the good of those who love him, who have been called according to his purpose."

Chapter Three
Shattered Heart Recovering Mind
Your Spirit is Free

It's the end of your life and it cuts like a knife
There are lots of things you will no longer do
There were lots of things you hated
which you'll no longer have to go through

You will no longer have to have chemotherapy or
radiotherapy which you hated so much
But now your suffering is over
I can no longer massage you
and you can't experience my touch

You don't have to visit your
Oncologist or Neurologist any more
You will no longer have so much
time away from home
in hospital like you did before

There is no more medication
that you will need to take
When it destroyed your bones
it made my heart ache

But you left a huge gap in my heart
the day you died and from us you had to depart
You no longer have to spend
so much time in your bed

Why Are You So Beautiful, Our Precious Angel?

You're not stuck with the memories of what
you used to be able to do in your head
That is of little comfort to me
At least now your spirit has been set free
You will never again experience sorrow
Nor will you have any seizures tomorrow
You will never feel anger
Never feel pain
Never experience how hard it is
to live in the world again
I believe one day you will be happy, joyful
Where every tear will be wiped away
I believe your life will be complete
I believe you will have the thrill of
kneeling at Jesus' feet

This has brought me comfort. It is something that will always provide reassurance and peace for me. What a glorious day when I am reunited in heaven with my son.

Psalm 46v1(NIV)
"God is our refuge and strength an ever-present help in trouble"

He Will Be In Heaven

I believe that in Heaven he will have joyous times
with our God the Father
I believe in heaven he will not feel sad
frustrated angry or mad
I believe there will be no more sorrow
no more pain
I believe there he will not be faced with the
pressures that we live in this world again

Revelations 21v 3-4 (NIV)

"And I heard a voice from heaven saying, "Now the dwelling of God is with men, and he will have with them. They will be his people, and God himself will be with them and be their God. He will wipe away every tear from their eyes. There will be no more death or mourning or crying or pain, for the old order of things has passed away."

Aiden's Not Coming Home

Aiden's dog greeted us excitedly
He was happy that we were all home
Aiden wasn't with us so
he continually went out on his own

Unfortunately he wasn't able
to be at the hospital when he died
Harry was expecting him to come home alive
The dog was expecting to jump on our bed
Aiden and Harry were really good friends

If this was a person, there are
lots of things that could have been said
There were dirty footprints
all over the floorboards of our house
When we cleaned up the mess
I really must confess
I decided it was a rotten experience
being home without our son

In and out the back door
Harry continually went
It was winter so my husband
was continually washing his paws
His patience and tolerance was
rapidly getting spent
It's hard with a dog
because they are unable to speak

Harry would have laid down next to Aiden
He's a Spoodle so his fur did not shed

Why Are You So Beautiful, Our Precious Angel?

He would have stayed by his side
all day and night comforting him
as he always did when our boy
was at his sickest until he died.
Harry would have snuggled up to us sadly
as he witnessed us all cry

Dogs are like children
Their devotion loyalty love
faithfulness honesty trust
He helped us to heal
Understood what we would feel
The devotion he had for his sisters' brother
is a valuable lesson
on how we should love one another

Romans 14v8 (NIV)

If we live, we live to the Lord: and if we die we die to the Lord. So, whether we live or die, we belong to the Lord."

Ephesians 4v2-4

"Be completely humble and gentle; be patient, bearing with one another in love. Make every effort to keep the unity of the Spirit through the bond of peace. There is one body and one Spirit just as you were called – one Lord, one faith, one baptism; one God and Father of all, who is over and through all and in all."

Adjustments and Emptiness

The mattress that was in our room is rarely used and behind
a closed door
I have to adjust to lying in bed with George without our son
like I did almost two and a half years before
Every night I'm lying in bed where our son used to be
It upsets me so much I often lie in bed and cry
Although George gives me lifesaving cuddles it just feels
so wrong
I'm trying to sleep in a spot where I feel our son belongs

In certain areas he is struggling with similar issues to me
We both need to learn and accept and respect that
we are grieving differently from one another
That is not a bad reflection on how much we need to
support
and continually show our love for each other

We are both up all night as he too is unable to see
why our son had to go against the natural order of things
There are certain times of the day or night
when we both find it harder to cope
Most of the time our worst feelings are
not connected with the same hours
That's probably a good thing because
otherwise I wouldn't give our marriage much hope
of surviving after what our son's illness
put our marriage through.

Jesus, I thank you that throughout Aiden's whole illness you were always there. I am grateful and thankful that he was wrapped up in this beautiful bubble of protection, and he was happy and healthy, most of the time, before he was diagnosed with cancer. I thank you that he was always grateful and thankful, under all circumstances. I thank you that he had such a close relationship with you. I thank you that nothing that anyone can do, will ever be able to separate us from your love.

Romans 8v38-39

"For I am convinced that neither death nor life, neither angels nor demons, neither the present nor the future, nor any powers, neither height nor depth, nor anything else in all creation, will ever be able to separate us from the love of God that is in Christ Jesus our Lord."

Why Are You So Beautiful, Our Precious Angel?

Unbearable Pain

My son has just died
Today I just spent a lot of time
in my room and cried

My brain feels numb and Jesus,
I need to spend some time alone with you
I'm really upset now
It's just so difficult dealing with this
massive pain that I have to go through

My girls needed me to spend more time with them today
In my room all day long is where I needed to stay
Tonight I will have quality time with them again
We are all grieving together
I treasure our quality time with each other
I just wish it could have been different
I wish we could have gone out with our daughters' brother

I'm glad they'll be home for four weeks
I'll spend more time with them and I'll
love and treasure them as long as I live

Philippians 4v7 (NIV)

And the peace of God,
Which transcends all understanding,
Will guard your hearts and minds
In Christ Jesus

Why Are You So Beautiful, Our Precious Angel?

Why Did This Have To Happen?

We have to go back to living with two children instead of
three
Sometimes when I'm feeling sorry for myself I think:
Why did this have to happen to me?
Several times a day I ask whilst crying:
Why is it my beautiful child had to go through
the suffering of dying?
Why did he end up so sick?
Why did he end up with a tumour in his head?
Why can't he run around like my daughters instead?
Why was he unable to go to school
or play in the park or swim in the pool?

Why did he die at only aged nine?
Why couldn't I have raised this child of mine?
Why weren't my husband and I able to fix this?
To have him healthy and running around now
would be pure bliss

Why couldn't I take all of his sickness away?
Why wasn't I left unable to drive?
It would have been worth it if our son was alive
Why couldn't our son be set free?
Why did this happen to him and not me?

Why couldn't the chemotherapy and radiotherapy work?
What was to be gained by having a tumour in his head?
Why did he get so sick he had to spend so much time in
bed?

Why Are You So Beautiful, Our Precious Angel?

Why did he have one year of really good quality life?
Why was he unable to grow up
get a girlfriend have a child and a wife?
Why did we get so little time with our son?
Why is it his battle could not be won?

Why did we have to bury our son?
Tell me why do we all have to grieve so much?
Why is he not around to kiss cuddle and touch
Why do we have to get used to living with only four?
Why can't there be five in the family like before?

Why do I have to witness the family go through so much pain?
Why do we get so upset when only five of us remain?
When will the pain ease from the chunk that left my heart?
When will the open wound start to close
after supporting him as he departed?

Jesus, I lift up to you anybody else who has just lot their child, from a terminal illness. I ask that they feel the peace and love that you give which surpasses all human understanding, and I ask that anybody that knew Aiden would feel your peace and love also. I lift up our family as they are trying to adjust to living without a brother and a son.

Death is a normal part of life
My grieving of him would come to an end
He will be in the loving arms of God
Father Protector God and Friend

Isiah 9 verse 6 (NIV)
"For to us a child is born, to us a son is given, and the government will be on his shoulders. And he will be called Wonderful, Counsellor, Mighty God, Everlasting Father, Prince of Peace"

Why Are You So Beautiful, Our Precious Angel?

A Mother's Love

I don't know how other parents cope
when their only child sadly and unfortunately dies
I don't know how they can have enough hope
after their special one is no longer alive
How does anybody stay strong
when the house is so quite
It's so wrong that things don't work out in this world

I don't know what I'd do without my girls
They are what I'm most proud of and love in this world
They will one day make beautiful mothers and wives

Losing your loved ones makes your priorities change
To have a quiet house now would really seem strange
We have to adjust to our son's death somehow

But we have two beautiful girls who also went through this tragedy
How do you cope while knowing?
there are no more children living with you
in your immediate family
That you can love watch see them learning and growing?

Jesus I ask you to hold my family today as I have spent a lot of time crying with you, and I pray that they will be able to talk to you not just as a God, but also as a loving friend who cares for them.

Why Are You So Beautiful, Our Precious Angel?

Isiah 26 verse 3 (NIV)

"You will keep in perfect peace him whose mind is steadfast, because he trusts in you"

Body and Spirit

I don't believe in karma and I'll tell you why.
Our courageous loving child did not deserve to die
There is nothing Aiden did to warrant him going through almost a third of his life being so sick
His family that were left behind suffered with him
We who are still grieving need something different to believe in
I don't believe in reincarnation or any other gods because God created the world, Adam and Eve, the universe as well
He even created heaven and hell

I don't believe that people are weighed down by any physical, Spiritual, intellectual or psychological illnesses in heaven

I believe Aiden's Heavenly father will raise him with:
Peace like he has never known,
Unconditional love because of his love for us,
Happiness and joy because I believe there is no misery in the next life.
I believe he will not be grieving because his joy will be so great
I believe Aiden will not feel any heartache.

Exodus 20 verse 3 (NIV)

"You shall have no other gods before me"

Why Are You So Beautiful, Our Precious Angel?

Philippians 3v20-21 (NIV)

"But our citizenship is in heaven. And we eagerly await a saviour from there, the Lord Jesus Christ, who, by the power that enables him to bring everything under his control, will transform our lowly bodies so that they will be like his glorious body."

The Dreaded Funeral

The dreaded day finally came
for us as a family to pay tribute to our beloved son.
Yesterday I saw our child in the coffin for the first time
as I'm not seeing his body today I'll be just fine
As a family we wrote down happy memories of our
beautiful boy

Pre-sickness he was a very cheeky one who was
full of mischief personality and really fun
When a video was shown that our daughter had made
I don't think there was a dry eye in the room
I was relieved I didn't have to get up and talk real soon

After the speech which I presented on that day
Fatigue slowly drained my energy away
Friends and family supported us
They were right by our side
As we grieved and cried
I was strong supportive and loving
I did what I needed to do
Something I would not wish
My worst enemy to have to go through

Why Are You So Beautiful, Our Precious Angel?

When we arrived I went straight to bed
I had such an intense pain in my head
I got up later and had take away food which I couldn't taste
It only got eaten so that it didn't go to waste
We comforted each other
We were all missing Aiden who was a nephew,
Grandson, son and brother

Jesus, I lift up my family now and I pray they will have the strength and endurance to be able to get through today. I am grateful that our eldest daughter made a video of happy memories that everyone at the funeral was able to look at.

I remember being in church one day and the chaplain said: "Why are you here?" and he said, in a big loud voice, without hesitation, "Because I like it."

His faith was so strong even though he was dying. I don't think the Chaplain will ever forget him saying that. It was something he mentioned at his funeral. Aiden really loved Jesus, God and he had a beautiful relationship with The Holy Spirit.

On the day of his funeral his paediatrician was there, and I thanked him for coming. He thanked me for letting him know about the funeral. He was grateful to able to be there and meet Aiden's relatives and friends.

Matthew 18 verse 5 (NIV)
"And whoever welcomes a little child like this in my name welcomes me"

Why Are You So Beautiful, Our Precious Angel?

No Happy Endings

We openly sobbed as the coffin went into the ground
We didn't care who witnessed this as we only had
close family and friends around
Words can't express how it felt to watch this visual
reminder
Which left us as a family temporarily in a complete mess
The stress puts the dynamics of our family unit through a
tougher test
His grandparents felt a different type of pain
According to them being the eldest it was their turn to go
first
There was no dirt covering the most beautiful boy in the
world
There they stood reasonably healthy and on this earth to
remain
Things will never be the same
My body couldn't go into denial in order to function
as a wife and mother again
It's indescribable to talk about feelings when in his coffin
My son's body will always remain

Lots of people brought flowers which were to go over the
dirt
But understanding that the coffin would get covered up
later
Made my feelings get hurt

God I thank you that you loved us before we were even
born. I thank you that you created us out of love. I pray for

all those people that have had to bury their own child today. I pray also for my own family as they watch their son, grandson nephew and brother get buried. I believe that you cried to when Aiden died. I believe that you also cry when you watch other peoples babies or children die. I believe that you understand how I feel, because I believe that your son Jesus died on the cross and you watched him die to. I believe that you also watched him get buried. I believe that you will rejoice when your children enter the kingdom of heaven.

Matthew 18v4 (NIV)
"Therefore, whoever humbles himself like this child is the greatest in the kingdom of heaven"

Why Are You So Beautiful, Our Precious Angel?

A Dog's Intuition

Harry no longer runs backwards when people come over
He was indifferent as to whether they were drunk or sober
If he knows them it's okay for them to give him a pat
He doesn't mind anyone coming over for a cuppa or a chat

When our son lived in this life
We could have the same palliative care doctor
Come to see Aiden each week or fortnight
Their attentions he would oppose to seek
He would bark run backwards and hide under his bed
If he could talk I'm sure he would say,
"Go away and let me look after him instead"

When Aiden was lying down
Frequently with bad seizures
Harry would go next to him and lick his face
He knew what he wanted to do
And would not leave him alone
Until he'd tried to pull him through
Harry would lie next to him for a cuddle
Every night he would sleep under his bed
When his dog was circling around his head
It meant our family expected trouble
It often meant Aiden's steroids had to be increased
Because of among other things inflammation to the brain
Or alternatively the seizures would again
Be so far out of control
That it might mean another stay in hospital again

Why Are You So Beautiful, Our Precious Angel?

I have so much admiration and respect for this dog
He cared for him comforted him Harry demonstrated unconditional love.
An example set by God who made the stars up above

I can remember many times when Aiden had seizures Harry would circle Aiden's head and lick his face to try and stop them. There were times when he would circle his face before he even had one. We always knew that when Harry was really concerned about Aiden, he needed to have his steroids increased.

I thank you God for creating animals, and I thank you that Harry was created in such a way, that he could smell seizures. I thank you that Harry was such a good friend to Aiden when he was sick.

Genesis 1v25 (NIV)

"God made the wild animals according to their kinds, the livestock according to their kinds, and all the creatures that move along the ground according to their kinds. And God saw that it was good."

Why Are You So Beautiful, Our Precious Angel?

Putting On a Brave Face

My brother and sister in law came over
And they ended up staying for lunch
I did not know how I would feel when
they came over, but when I saw them
I really enjoyed their company
They were patient, kind and drove a long way to get here
Which left me feeling touched

They had made a big pot of pumpkin soup
And we all did some cooking as well
In the moments when I accepted the truth
My mind went through turmoil and I fell
into the old routine of going into the room where Aiden had slept
I was happy when I was in denial as a coping mechanism
I wept when I saw the bed was empty
I had even set up an extra place on the table
where he used to sit
with God's help I am able to enjoy the company of my
brother and sister in law
that I love so much
She is my sister from another mother
He is my much loved brother
I appreciated them, respected them
Knew how much they cared
It was good that they came so that we could eat together

Jesus, I lift up my brother and sister in law today and I pray that they will feel your peace.

John 15v13 (NIV)

"Greater love has no one than this, that he lay down his life for his friends."

Job 12 verse 13 (NIV)

"To God belong wisdom and power counsel and understanding are his"

Disappointment

My daughter was supposed to go on camp yesterday,
One that was funded by a charity
However, she got sick and was unable to go.
She didn't throw any tantrums, get angry, cry or ask why
She simply said, in a way that made me realise,
I didn't need to talk to her or get it through her head
All she said was, "I don't want to be responsible for another child to die"
She said that because she didn't want a child or family
to go through pneumonia after a cold which killed her brother
If someone got sick because of her, she wouldn't know what to do
Although the people at camp would have cared,
They wouldn't have appreciated her being there

She had stomach cramps, headaches, migraines as well as the flu
I thought at one stage she might have meningitis
Which is something she didn't deserve to go through
I shouldn't have been in this situation where my daughters could go on camps for free
I still feel sorry for myself, because I'm upset that this had to happen to be

She has over five years where she can go on camps, get spoilt and have fun
Where she can be accepted as the number one goal for the short holiday
Is to allow her to be a treasured child, who can really live and play

Why Are You So Beautiful, Our Precious Angel?

My daughter would be accepted as she deserves the very best in life

I just wish she would've been well enough to go away that day

Jacinta is a credit to us for her strength, love and trust
She was a credit to the camp organisers, that she did this on her own,
not for them or us She demonstrated kindness, pure selflessness respect and care for other families with children who were suffering with chronic illnesses
I was so proud of her then, I really loved her and I still love her.

Deuteronomy 6 verse 5:

"Love the Lord your God, with all your heart and with all your soul and with all your strength"

Why Are You So Beautiful, Our Precious Angel?

Love/Heartache/Friendship

We received a phone call, from a family friend,
Asking us gently to come over.
I knew then sadly, that it was because his wife's time,
In this life had come to, or was coming to an end.

I cried when I saw her, and I'll tell you why,
She was another victim, of this hideous disease, cancer.
It robbed my son, from his much deserved, quality of life.
In a different, but equally demeaning way,
It stole from this cherished woman, who will be greatly missed,
as she was a loving, supportive friend and wife.
A selfish part of me thought, not at this moment,
I'm too raw, to be dealing with this right now.
I need to find the inner strength
To put my grievances aside, and adjust to this pain somehow.

While we are grieving, angry and sad,
She's no longer in pain now, and I believe she will enjoy spending time with her loved ones I believe she will spend time with her like minded brothers and sisters in Christ
I believe she will no longer get mad because she will be happy in the arms
of God who is her heavenly provider father and friend
Her husband was not ready, to stop reassuringly,
And sportively, lovingly nurturing her.
Taking her home from hospital, better or well on the Road to recovery, is what he would have preferred.

Why Are You So Beautiful, Our Precious Angel?

Unfortunately cancer claimed another victim,
As this is a demeaning, viscous, hideous disease.
I'm tired of crying, as close friends, loved ones,
Or relatives, are sick or they're dying.
We desperately, need a cure for this now please.

While we were there, our friends brother,
Received a call on his mobile phone.
His sister was coming over, with her partner,
so he didn't have to spend the night alone.

They all went out to the local pub, to eat dinner together.
He was missing his wife, as he wanted, to remain with her forever

They honoured us by giving us the
Privilege of supporting them through her death
Something he was not ready to go through with yet

Jesus, I lift up our friend and I ask you to be with him and anyone else that knew and loved his wife. I thank you that she had a close relationship with you and that she loved you.

Ephesians 5v9-10 (NIV)

"(for the fruit of the light consists in all goodness, righteousness and truth)"
"And find out what pleases the Lord"

Matthew 6v9-13 (KJV)

"Our Father who is in heaven
Hallowed be your name
Your kingdom come, Your will be done
on earth, as it is in heaven.
Give us today our daily bread
And forgive us our debts,
as we also have forgiven our debtors
And do not lead us into temptation,
but deliver us from evil.
(For Yours is the kingdom and the power and
the glory for ever, amen.")

Surprising Strength through Extenuating Circumstances

I remember when Aiden had his second bout of pneumonia, a few months before he died. I was staying overnight in hospital with him and I came across a very familiar face. She had often been in the same ward as me, she with her daughter and me with my son. It never ceases to amaze me, how it can bring out the very best in people, who are going through worst situations then what you are.

The difference was that she did not have any other children. I asked her how her daughter was, even before she answered me, I could tell by the way her face changed and her eyes filled with tears that her daughter had died. With her head high, she was able to look me straight in the eyes and tell me how long ago this had happened.

The reason she was there, was because she had a friend

who was a single mum, with other children at home, so she was taking care of this very sick child. When I asked this amazing, highly intelligent, inspirational woman who was a very mature and reliable mother how she could do this, she told me that she wanted to do it and she needed to do it.

Unlike Aiden it had been more obvious right from the start that her daughter was going to be spending all of her life in and out of hospital. It made me feel sad that this innocent, young, precious soul had not experienced the same quality of life that Aiden did, up until a month before he was diagnosed. If this is what she is like to other people's children, what a compassionate mother she has been and what a strong supportive wife she obviously is.

The very next day she said goodbye and went to work. I have since lost contact with her, but it did cross my mind that she should be nominated for mother of the year award, because of her love and support for others, as well as her deep inner beauty. Had I not been so stressed as a result of my son's illness, I would have done this one small act of kindness, on her behalf, that she so richly deserved.

Conclusion

It hadn't occurred to me until after we were driving home from hospital, after saying our final goodbyes to our son, that the reason he was placed in a larger area was so that we as a family could spend our last night in the same room together with Aiden. He had spent five nights in a smaller room, not big enough for more than one parent to be staying overnight, let alone his two sisters who were really struggling both in different ways, with what was happening to their brother.

George had called me in the early hours on Saturday morning, to inform me that they were being moved very soon. Later on that day, I had mentioned to Sharna and Jacinta that we would all be spending the night at the hospital, because there was a possibility that their brother might not be coming home.

I was not fully able to accept how correct I would be when talking to our other daughters. Neither girl was able to process properly what I was trying to tell them. How do you prepare the other siblings with things like that, when it's too hard to face it yourself?

I sat in the car thinking, while my brain was numb with shock and I remember it had been difficult to walk out, knowing that I would never be able to take my son home again. This was it, the dreaded final goodbyes that all the medical staff had been talking about for over twelve months. I was relieved that my husband had the strength to drive home, because I probably would have crashed the car. I was too exhausted on the way home to cry. I felt protected

Why Are You So Beautiful, Our Precious Angel?

and loved when he drove home, because I realised how hard it would have been for him to do this.

One of the first things that I did when I got home from the hospital, was to go through all of his medications, that had had so many detrimental side effects, among other things, making his bones brittle. I needed to make a phone call, as I had forgotten what was to be thrown out and what was to go to the chemist, for the pharmacist to deal with.

There was just one more thing I needed to do, before I was able to sit down and have a strong cup of tea. I decided to remove all of my son's toys and books from beside the bed so that they weren't there to torture me when it was time to escape into sleep. I walked into Aiden's room and had to remind myself that he had not slept there for two and a half years. I sobbed uncontrollably for what seemed like a very long time. Aiden's things ended up inside his walk in robe, with the door closed, so that I didn't have to face seeing them.

I remember lying in bed with George and feeling loved and reassured, because he just cuddled me. It was what I really needed at the time, and I was grateful and thankful to receive and feel that support. It was a blessing to be able to cuddle him back as we were both grieving.

If you are reading this and you know somebody that has lost a child, through a terminal illness, then it's important to ask them what it is that they need. Let them know, that you are there if you need them, and remind them that it's okay for them to contact you in this difficult time.

Encourage that person or people to get counselling, or talk things over with their local minister.

Eighty per cent of couples divorce after the loss of a child, so if they don't contact you much it could mean that they are trying to resolve conflict within their own marriage. It could also mean that they are needing time as a family to readjust to the new meaning of being a family, and working at their marriage, so they need a lot of family time.

For a single mum she will have her own challengers which she will be facing, which is just as difficult, but she will still have the financial burdens as well.

For somebody that is really strong in their faith, it may mean that they need to spend time alone with God so that they can heal and feel his love and presence. People have so many different coping mechanisms and grieving processes when they lose somebody that is close to them.

It may be helpful to encourage them to have couple counselling. If there are remaining siblings, it may be appropriate and helpful to respectfully and lovingly suggest that if the parents discuss the importance and value of having counselling to help them to move on from the loss of their brother/sister.

One thing that really helped us was one of the ladies from the funeral provided a holiday for us for one week. Things like that are really valuable. Things like making meals and providing financial support in the ways of paying bills and being available to walk with them and lovingly support them through their pain, can be very beneficial for a family that's recovering. They will be in shock for a while and that's normal, in particular if it is a sudden death like a car accident and the parent/parents have not had the time to say goodbye.

Everybody has different ways of expressing themselves and different needs when it comes to losing their child.

For me what gave me comfort during our son's illness and after he died, was knowing that he had faith in God. Even though he never developed a lot of language I could see and feel his relationship with Jesus, because of the way that he accepted it and even though he got angry sometimes, he did not hold onto it. He always dealt with each day as it came and did not talk about what was going to happen in the future.

If you suspect that the person you are supporting, is not coping very well then they may need extra support, and there are plenty of places that a person can go to if they need to.

Suicide Helpline	1300 651 251
Lifeline	13 11 14
Mensline	1300 789 978
Griefline (noon to 3am)	(03) 9596 7799
Kids Help Line	1800 55 1800
(5 - 25 years)	

Why Are You So Beautiful, Our Precious Angel?

Susan was unprepared for the disaster which would befall her and her family. As family and friends surrounded the family there was still grief to resolve, to heal from. The art of poetry became a place of solace and restoration for Susan. Through each failure of modern medicine to bring ongoing healing to her son, the author pens inner thoughts, continual hope and depth of love for her dying son.

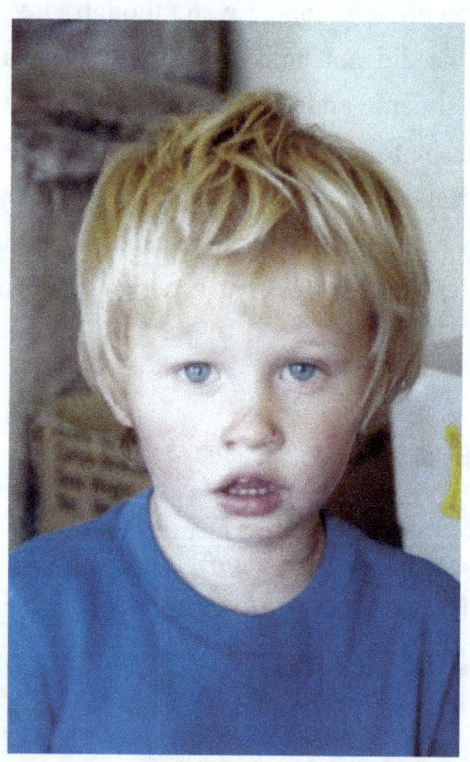